T0124439

# LOVE & POEMS

Sunny Monroe

authorHOUSE®

*AuthorHouse™*
*1663 Liberty Drive*
*Bloomington, IN 47403*
*www.authorhouse.com*
*Phone: 833-262-8899*



*Published by AuthorHouse 09/05/2023*

*ISBN: 979-8-8230-1399-4 (sc)*
*ISBN: 979-8-8230-1395-6 (e)*

*Library of Congress Control Number: 2023916871*

*Print information available on the last page.*



*This book is printed on acid-free paper.*

*"And we have known and believed the love that God hath to us. God is love; and he that dwelleth in love, dwelleth in God, and God in him."*

*1 John 4 KJV*

# CONTENTS

# EMOTIONS

*Why do I feel all these emotions; I feel all these like the flow of the ocean, the waves keep going as far as I can see; like my emotions are deeper than me, keep thinking why I'm sad, happy, angry, mad; I can't be scared these are just normal I'm glad, but still why all these emotions, I love you: can you understand why my love for you is true, I just want to control my emotions all the way now; but soon I will be able to and now I know how.*

# TRUST

*Trust is earned not given; Trust will make a person driven,*
*Trust is not to be taken lightly; Trust doesn't yield not at all*
*slightly; Trust will stop you in your path; Trust will make you feel*
*Gods wrath, Trust is not fake or phoney; Trust will make*
*you recount your money, Trust is worthy doesn't slack;*
*Trust will make you break a persons' back. For real.*

## HALF-ASS

*My love is not half ass; when I look at you, I've already forgotten my past, I see in your eyes your mine; for sure real love takes its time, that's okay because I'm willing to stay; as long as you will too okay.*

# TO MY EVERYTHING

*How do I begin, my everything that is you; it's not easy to give*
*my heart but it's overdue, I knew you were the one for me;*
*soon the world will see you and me together as One; don't be*
*afraid love it's done, no more searching I'm here now; my one and only,*
*the love of my life wow, I'm happy I have found you, my everything*
*I will keep loving; no matter what wonderful you my hubby.*

# FAITH

*What is faith; is it something you can escape, Faith is embedded in me; but sometimes it's tested I get weak, Faith is not hidden behind a door; I don't want to deal with this no more, where is my Faith, where is my belief; I don't want to step to far too deep, I want to believe in Faith, Hope, Love, it is real; is it like the stars up above, I hope Faith never leaves me; I just know I can't leave it, but it makes me weep, Faith is tattooed on my chest; I don't know how to explain the rest, that shit hurts like word; I just know I can't give up on myself your heard.*

## LOSE MYSELF

*As I sit here and dream about you; I lose myself in my dreams too, I wish you were here and I know you're coming soon, I love you baby, it's forever me and you.*

## LOVE TO ME IS?

*A flower in a rose garden; not to be touched by anyone pardon, me I'm minding my own business here I am love only to pick me when you are ready; love to me is well, a slow but steady love, not to be rushed but savored slowly like ribs cooking on a grill, now that's love to me.*

## LOSE CONTROL

*I lose control I am lost without you baby; come to me baby I love you deeply, can't survive without you beside me; I don't know why I feel so lost suffering quietly, I smile every day on the outside; but I am hurting on the inside, please my love answer me don't leave; for I am losing control and can't breathe.*

# TOGETHER

*I know we be together soon; I love you from the sun to the moon, let's keep this fire going forever; soon I know we will be together, I Love you, baby.*

## CLOCK TICKING

*As the clock ticks by; I can't wait to come to you and say hi, that's means everyday time flies away; I know it's us getting closer to the day, that I'm in your arms forever; and never, ever leaving you it's us together.*

# I'M WAITING

*Still waiting on you not to be mistaken for a fool; okay I see you*
*but I'm waiting because I love you, touch me baby here*
*and forever; never leave me love no matter what endeavors*
*you encounter, yes my baby it's nothing like your love; I need*
*it, want it so bad like a dove, swimming in the lake looking for food; oh*
*yes, touch me love do it to me, I love you can you feel me, cause I can*
*feel you, whisper sweet in my ear; all I want here is you my dear.*

## MISS YOU

*I miss you so much and I wish you were here with me;*
*I don't know how the next chapter is going to be, I just*
*know that I want you right beside me you see.*

# DEEP

*Sometimes I'm deep in my thoughts not for the faint of heart;*
*but I want to get caught, loving you saying it for the world*
*who knew, that it is me and you too, until the end boo are you*
*here with me, I get nervous not because of you but because of*
*abandonment you see, I hope you come back baby and be with me,*
*I'm lost without you, I can't without you, stop me baby I*
*can go on and on about you, I hope this reaches you, teaches*
*you that my arms are empty and without you.*

# NEVER LOVED LIKE THIS

*I have never loved like this before; I'm afraid to open up once*
*more, afraid of being hurt, abandoned and disappointed*
*again; are you really my man, or is it just another thing for*
*you to do; not thinking about how you affect the other person*
*because of your ego too, baby you have no idea how old that*
*gets but one day you will boo, so let's be grown about what we do and how we*
*really should love someone; you keep up with this bull I will be gone and done.*

# TO MY LOVER

*To my lover I shall return to you; not someday but soon, I miss you terribly and can't continue to consume this emptiness; I hope wherever you are you know this, not for many people to understand my love for you; it's okay though me and you know what's true, so to my lover I say this; never, ever lose that feeling for me as I count the days that we kiss.*

# I WILL LEAVE

*I will leave if you're not with me; I will leave because I can't hurt no more you see; I will leave not for you but for me okay; I will leave for my peace of mind every day; I will leave you because your rude; I will leave you in a split second, now what you gonna do; I will leave if this is a game; I will leave you now but your life will never be the same.*

# LOVE

*Love what is it really though; fast, slow sorry my love is*
*overwhelming but seriously there's no love like mine; my love is*
*real not the kind you used to getting when people want to*
*steal your love, because it's free; kisses, hugs you know and you see, it's*
*okay to love someone but protecting yourself always is who I want to be.*

# LEAD WITH YOUR MIND

*When you lead with your mind and not your heart, your eyes are open wide; it's not easy but I tried, it's easy to say but not to do; love hurts but yet we aren't honest too, don't be fooled by the heart it will get you every time; blind you so you don't see the truth in leading with your mind.*

# HOLD TIGHT

*Hold tight my dear; real tight have no fear, it's going to be a journey we have to go through; hold tight though God is not through with you, it may seem hard day by day, especially at night when you are in your thoughts; but just know who's in control always no thoughts, never question his way; for sure he got us, remember day by day, so when you feel tired and you can't hold tight, God is right next to you holding you with all his might.*

## YOU

*It's not a day that goes by that I don't see you next to me; like the stars in the sky, like the ocean as deep as the sea; it's you I see next to me.*

# THROUGH THE FIRE

*As I gaze into your eyes; I start to cry but not sad tears, my dear*
*but happiness without fear, I don't want to go through*
*the fire with no one else; but I understand that relationships*
*change like the seasons do, well there's winter, summer, spring and*
*fall but nothing is most important to me but what's right here next*
*to me; you baby, so through the fire we go let's last forever, I know*
*that I want to gaze into your eyes as we grow old together.*

# MISS YOU

*I miss you so much and I wish you were here with me; I don't know how the next chapter for me is going to be, I just know that I want you right beside me you see.*

# SAD BUT TRUE

*Sad but true like the song says; don't you understand what it*
*means anyway well let me explain, now you don't want to see*
*the truth; now or in the future you got to believe what's do and overdue,*
*keep waiting for you and it's been a year; what makes you think you are not*
*disposable my dear, just saying sad but true let's go further okay; for real it's*
*not me wasting my time in you every day but me learning how you move in*
*stressful times today, it's my future to be with you because I love you;*
*but don't get it twisted I love you yes, and I will leave you too.*

# END OF SUMMER

*As the summer is passing and the leaves are falling; our love is growing stronger and stronger my dear and you calling me your wife soon; how many times I have to say I love you a million times, times 2 forever me and you.*

# MY ENERGY

*My energy is not like others; sometimes quiet and at times happy, energy is not something you take for granted; only given once in this life and how you can manage, when is it enough for people to use your energy for themselves; take it and keep it for themselves, they are not worth a damn my energy is not free; I have lots of energy inside of me, so don't just give your energy to anyone; but give your energy to someone.*

# SEASONAL FRIENDS

*Yeah, friends are seasonal too, they come and go; but true friends stay you know, not just for a season but until the end of time; people have seasonal friends since high school or even lived in the same neighborhood for years too, in good and bad times; through thick and thin, laughter and tears, yet throughout the years your friend circle gets smaller, maybe it's change or people become shallow, seasonal friends sometimes is good; because now you know who is willing to stay with you as they should.*

# RELATIONSHIPS COME IN SEASONS

*Relationship comes in seasons; just like spring, fall, winter and summer, one day a person is all for you; the next day they trying to cut you true, people wear different faces; but when they are exposed, now they catching cases, children, family, coworkers are all relationships we have; but one by one they slowly disappear like the seasons do; believe it one day and the next one is you.*

## HANDS

*My love I love you; I will reach out my hand to you and touch yours and hold it for life, my beloved forever.*

# MINDSET

*Change your mindset and see changes in your life; when you change the mind, the body follows right, it's easy to say but hard to do; you not alone and we all in it too, the universe is moving fast; not waiting for anyone let's see how long you last, if you don't change your mindset, I bet you this times next year or sooner, you going to wish you did it with regret.*

# TRUTH BE TOLD

*Yes, so the truth be told; but I remember when I was growing up*
*the truth was not told, instead there were lies, deceit and*
*fairy tales; but as I got older I saw the truth about the lies but*
*oh well, now looking back on that and knowing how to*
*navigate through the fiction; why are my eyes still closed now,*
*not because of the truth but because of addiction.*

# DARKEST DAYS

*In the darkest days there is a light just behind the stars; that light up in the sky including mars, love wins but in those darkest days the light is still there; it seems far away but together it's the love we share, so let's keep fighting through the darkest days; as one day the darkness goes all away.*

# LISTEN TO ME

*I'm hurting too the pain is real; it's hard to explain to you so*
*okay here's the deal, I need you so badly I can taste it; but this*
*distance is deep I can't fake it, when you got sick I fell to my*
*knees, prayed every day for your healing and now I say, I want*
*to get back to us like it used to be; but recently it hasn't been*
*you and me, the disease, illness, sickness that's the focus now;*
*I'm here and always will be but sometimes I don't know how to*
*be, I'm not there; but if it was up to me, your wife, partner to*
*be, I would be there, this is new for me, your wife; listen to me as I cry*
*for you my dear, it's not just you hurting it's me too can you hear.*

# DON'T LET ME GO

*Don't let me go I see you; time is passing by I'm choosing you, I'm here and you there I can't keep up; what's up baby you everywhere, but be still for once I need you with me; this keep spinning around in my head don't you agree, the love we have is fast and furious speeding, don't you ever sit back and say I'm curious and needy on how he loves me why; okay maybe I shouldn't say why, but I try to love you, don't ever let me go never; for our love with each other is strong together.*

# TRUE LOVE PT. 1

*True love doesn't lie; true love doesn't ask why, true love forgives but never forgets; true love has no regrets, true love is patient, gentle and kind; true love is definitely hard to find, true love doesn't play; true love will hold you and say it will be okay, true love stays up at night waiting for you; true love gets mad but stays true, true love will be by your side; but don't ever take for granted true love it's true but doesn't come around often people ask why; they say, if true love isn't nurtured, protected and loved; then true love goes away.*

# WHAT'S LOVE WITHOUT PATIENCE

*What's love without patience; simply love that strong but*
*vulnerable, peaceful but loud, I'm proud to be in love, loving*
*someone doesn't have a price tag; but love is to embrace in the*
*moment without limits, patience is hard to have no lie, but*
*what's love without patience is something we should all try,*
*what's love without patience some people turn away, run but do you feel*
*the same about love or will you turn your back on it and give up.*

# I WONDER

*I wonder if I wouldn't have never answered that message; I wonder if I would have ignored your response will I still be guessing, I wonder if I would have given up and walked away; I wonder and I'm happy that I didn't listen to my thoughts, I stayed, I wonder if I didn't go through that situation my dear; I wonder that and know it's God that brought me to you my love with no fear, now that we have found each other, I wonder no more baby you are my greatest lover.*

## I STAY

*I stay because I believe you are telling me the truth; I stay because I love you, I stay because I see a future in your eyes; I stay because we connect beautifully, I stay because I'm lost without you; I stay because our love is deep and true, I stay because we make love passionately; I stay because we belong together, I stay because we are spiritually connected.*

# LOVE YOU AS MUCH

*I love you as much as I do because who knew; you would win*
*the lottery with a winner well I'm not through, hmm not a*
*celebrity style but the real stuff hungry no bull; hungry for real love*
*does it exist, I'm full of love that I'm ready to give to you,*
*love you as much as I do, yeah it's hard I'm not with*
*you every day yet; but soon my dear we be together no*
*texting, let's not forget what got us here I'm ready.*

# NOTHING MORE

*There is nothing more I would love but to kiss you and hold your hands; not like the fairytales but real touching you understand, I know it's possible to do this as you let me don't fight it; I'm not a threat, don't be scared of me, our love is our strength and motivation; yes, I meant that with our situation and also our creation a love that is true to heart I have nothing more to say but I don't ever want to be apart.*

# STRONG BOND

*My love, we have a strong bond; like glue on wood we connect like two people in love should, our love will go beyond measures; for you my dear I will always treasure, your love for me is higher than the stars in the sky; my love for you will always rise, rise up like the sun when it hits the earth like it's set in your eyes; I verily say, come with me my dear forever, hold my hand, let this bond lead us to the promise land; my love lets walk together as husband and wife but finally yes, baby as we planned for life.*

# UNIQUE

*Unique I am my own unique self; now not like someone whose plain so deaf, I'm unique in my own way; but now that I'm older I see my way, hmm maybe a poet someday and a famous one; I'm real for real since day one, I'm unique no magazine can change my story; when people read about me and my poems they will say this woman was unique but never boring.*

# MY FUTURE

*This is a letter to myself my future; the unknown, the abyss, just not knowing is me not her, my own destiny what I do now affects it; so I can slack, put off or even procrastinate oh shit, this is real not phoney time is passing by quickly; get it together now no bull not sticky, a thought is a dream, pen and paper is writing it down; but putting in work is going to town, so when you get discouraged, sad or want to give up; look up above God got you and remember where you started from and don't interrupt.*

## MY LOVE

*As God has bestowed his hands upon us; we will come together as one soon just us, I love you baby can you imagine I came to you in your sleep; I promise you when I do its going to be sweet.*

# HEART

*A heart contains two people's fingers connected not apart; without the other there is no heart, our hearts are one and I will always be connected to you my love, I love you baby and I carry your heart everywhere I go.*

# OH GOD!

*Oh God help me control my emotions; don't let me down I don't know how to swim like in the ocean, I feel lonely sometimes without you; I wish I could hear your voice again soon, I remember you spoke to me with a loud but stern sound; it woke me up out of my sleep so profound, I hear you God I need you so much; but I am trying, pleading, crying for you and your touch, Oh God comfort me in my need of sadness; please hold me tight with shear gladness; as I cry out for you daily; when I do hear you again I'm going to know it's you speaking even though people say I'm crazy.*

# DAD

*Dad where were you when I needed you, you left and never came back through, a little girl looking for you, now I got to settle for this hell; felt like prison here oh well, but without you, remember the laughs and the tears, dancing to the Commodores but now no more, shared a space with two other people you knew, you helped created too, but now looking around where are you, as I look out the window waiting for your return; fast forward 10 years later all that time has burned, so looking back now 25 years later what a lesson to be learned.*

# DON'T LET ME GO

*Don't let me go I see you; time is passing by I'm choosing you, I'm here and you there I can't keep up; what's up baby you everywhere, be still for once I need you with me; this keep spinning around in my head don't you agree, the love we have is fast and furious; speeding don't you ever sit back and say I'm curious, needy, on how he loves me why; okay maybe I shouldn't say why, but I try to love you, don't ever let me go never; for our love with each other is strong together.*

# STRENGTH IS REAL

*My strength is within me; only God can see my strength and*
*what is could be, my strength is valued; I value it can't wait*
*until this chapter starts maybe I can grasp it finally, well yeah*
*I realize my strength, not to brag on it but to take it in,*
*all of it day by day and that what's meant.*

## NOTHING MORE

*There is nothing more than I would love but to kiss you and hold your hands; not like a fairytale but real touching you understand, I know it's possible to do this as you let me don't fight it; I'm not a threat I just want to taste it, our love is our strength and motivation; yeah I meant that with our situation, and also our creation a love that is true to heart, I have nothing more to say; except I don't ever want to be apart.*

# FORGIVENESS

*I'm not the one to persecute someone for their mistakes; we are not perfect people but just wait, I want to say this, I know that you love me truly; forgiveness is not forgetting but allowing me to heal from the hurt you see, I believe you and that your heart is real; I know you wouldn't do anything to our love but still, I know that forgiving you my love is not hard; you know why because I can never see us apart. NEVER*

# I ONCED LOVED YOU

*I once loved you this is true; I gave you my all this is you know,
we cried together, laughed and disagreed; now that I know who
you really are I am free, you lied to me over and over
again that wasn't cool; I believed you yes, you were my dude but I played the
fool; I once loved you yes indeed, but karma a bitch and one day you will see.*

# ALL OF ME

*From the beginning I gave you all of me; when I first spoke to you I thought we were meant to be, I opened up my heart to you all of it, I wasn't expecting for you to leave me oh shit, the day you walked away, you hurt me a lot and I must say, now that time has gone by, I thank God now but I wonder why.*

# HAPPINESS

*All I ever wanted in life was happiness like hearing the birds sing in the spring, to feel free within myself; this is all I ever wanted this is how I felt but not looking for it in anyone else; you can't find happiness in anyone but yourself, what is the meaning of happiness, well to me its loving everything and my whole being.*

# WILD DREAMS

*My wild dreams came true when I met you; not made up or something in a magazine, but in my wildest dreams, like the snow is white every winter that falls out of the sky; sometimes I say to myself why, but not to doubt but to pinch myself without a doubt; this is real for me and for you; so now don't you believe you wildest dreams can come true.*

## SOULMATE

*You are my soulmate forever every day; not what you typically think a soulmate is in anyway, it's a bond and true connections to each other, I love you no matter what; no regrets or doubts for sure when I miss you I feel a part of me too gone; I'm your rib, partner, lover, soulmate and I can't wait to get my hands on you tonight babe, I swear I can't wait.*

# KEEP IT REAL

*As long as you keep it real with me, I will keep it real with you;*
*just as the sun goes down and the sky is blue, I don't ask for*
*much boo, I'm not picky, materialistic or bitchy; but I do*
*deserve all of you not half-ass this is true; I know relationships are not easy*
*to do but I love you and we can fight together as one but if you betray me*
*and lose my trust; well it's not going to end good for you because be dust.*

# TRUE LOVE PT. 2

*True love does not lie ask why, well I tell you it keep you in suspense; not intense but calm and easy and true love does not brag or boast, it's natural like the pacific coast; true love is when you find it, it finds you just like a good high heal shoe, true love is there when you hurt it doesn't leave you alone to cry; it will lift you up even when you don't want to try, so what is true love really true, we are all searching for that one thing and its True.*

# A MOTHERS LOVE

*A mothers' love is like no other love; one that's real and it fits*
*like a glove, a mothers' love doesn't cut corners; it's from the*
*heart need I say, I did warn you, she protects her babies like a*
*lions' cubs as she should; she gets out there and fight with you*
*tooth and nail, if you go to jail oh yeah, she got your bail, so be grateful she*
*loves you and she's there, she will whisper in your ear when you are asleep I*
*may not be there with you in the physical but we are never apart so don't weep.*

# PASSION

*Passion is what I feel when I'm with you; passion doesn't just stop it's always in me but I'm not threw, passion is inside of all of us; passion is love and lust, passion is deep and fulfilling; passion is sexual healing, passion is me touching you while you close your eyes; passion is me caressing you gently on your thighs, passion is love between two people who love each other; passion has no time, it's anytime, anyplace of the day with two or more lovers.*

# DEAR GOD

*Dear God, who is loving and caring; a strong being of force that's daring, yes this is who I worship and see, there are no other Gods but you to me; he can't be replaced, mocked or fooled; no matter what the world says to you about Him keep your cool, One God who I so love and has saved me; it doesn't matter what people say about Him one day they will see, that's he's the Almighty, the light for your darkness, the strength when you need him, this is what God is to whom believes.*

Printed in the United States
by Baker & Taylor Publisher Services